Praying
How to Start and Keep Going

Bobb Biehl

James W. Hagelganz

Regal Books
A Division of GL Publications
Ventura, CA 93006

The foreign language publishing of all Regal books is under the direction of GLINT. GLINT provides financial and technical help for the adaptation, translation and publishing of books in more than 85 languages for millions of people worldwide.

For more information write: GLINT, P.O. Box 6688, Ventura, CA 93006.

The Scripture quotations in this publication are from the following versions:

NASB *The New American Standard Bible.* © The Lockman Foundation 1960, 1962, 1963, 1968, 1971, 1972, 1973, 1975. Used by permission.

TLB *The Living Bible,* Copyright © 1971 by Tyndale House Publishers, Wheaton, Illinois. Used by permission.

NIV *The New International Version,* New Testament. Copyright © 1973 by New York Bible Society International. Used by permission.

Phillips *THE NEW TESTAMENT IN MODERN ENGLISH,* Revised Edition, J.B. Phillips, Translator. © J.B. Phillips 1958, 1960, 1972. Used by permission of the Macmillan Co., Inc.

KJV *King James Version*

Published by Regal Books
A Division of G/L Publications
Ventura, California 93006
Printed in U.S.A.

Library of Congress Catalog Card No. 80-54003
ISBN 0-8307-0781-6

Dedication

This book is dedicated to our wives,
Betty Hagelganz and Cheryl Biehl,
whose love for us is made more beautiful
through their faithful praying,
and to those whose praying
has influenced our lives.

Contents

Preface and
Prayer of Dedication

"I don't know how to pray. Can you help me?"

This frequent plea comes from people involved in many walks of life, and from just as many different churches. There is a lot of talk about praying, Christians are encouraged to pray, but that isn't enough. Our purpose in this book is to help you actually *experience* meaningful praying.

You can use this book in your personal, private praying, with a group of friends on a prayer retreat, or at a prayer meeting. You may be able to take a day away in personal retreat. Hopefully, you will find *Praying* flexible and expandable, according to your needs.

This book comes out of our personal experiences and convictions. The two of us, a minister and a layman, got together to share what we know and feel about praying. We wrote the book together and it speaks for both of us at every point. For the sake of readability and flow, when personal references are made, we do not stop to indicate whose experience is being described. All our experiences speak for both of us.

Here's how we put the book together.

Chapter 1 deals with just what praying is and why we should pray. Chapter 2 deals with the five essential facets of prayer: Praise, Confession, Thanksgiving, Petition, Intercession. All forms, or methods, of praying focus on one or more of these five facets—even conversational prayer and praying in the Spirit.

Each chapter deals with one of the facets and explains very simply its biblical, theological and practical elements. At the end of each chapter is a personal response section you can use in developing that facet of praying in your own prayer life.

Chapter 7 is entitled, "Your Praying Notebook: A Tool to Revolutionize Your Prayer Life." It offers suggestions and examples to help you develop your own praying notebook, something that could transform your life as a Christian.

Chapter 8 concludes the book with practical suggestions for overcoming obstacles and continuing to develop a prayer life that is more meaningful and fulfilling in every way.

Before you get started, we would like to stop—as they say—"for a word of prayer." Call it a prayer of dedication. Call it a prayer of hope and expectancy. Whatever it is, we believe it expresses what *Praying* is all about:

Heavenly Father,

Within this book help each reader experience more clearly what you are really like. Through *Praying* replace each reader's personal turmoil and pressures with your peace of mind as he realizes that you actually respond to his praying in your perfect love and complete power.

There is so much loneliness, Father, in hospital rooms, in broken marriages, in prison cells. Through *Praying* turn lonely hours into a time when the deepest of fears are transformed into the strongest of faith.

Father, with strengthened faith, through *Praying*, please help each reader find your answers to his pressing questions. Give him a new confidence of personal direction to replace any confusion and the strength to carry out the visions you give.

In the learning about you and experiencing of your love, please purify each of us with your forgiveness that we will be crystal clear, shiny clean, pure tools for your use.

Your will be done—to you be the glory! Draw each of us closer to yourself through *Praying*.

In the name of your Son, Jesus.
Amen!

CHAPTER ONE

Praying Is...

Praying is something we all talk about but it seems that few of us do enough of it. When we tested the title of this book on a considerable number of Christians they would reply: "That's what I need—something to help me get started." Or they would say, "I've started so many times; I need something to keep me going."

We hope *Praying: How to Start and Keep Going* will give you many practical ideas and tools for getting started in a meaningful prayer life *and* keep it going. But before we get into the practical

specifics—the major portion of the book—
we believe it's important to lay some foun-
dational principles. So, let's talk about just
what praying is . . . and what it is not.

**Praying Is More
than Just Words**

According to the Westminster Larger
Catechism, "Prayer is the offering up of our
desires unto God, in the name of Christ, by
the help of His Spirit." In straightforward
terms, prayer is simply talking with God—
and the simpler the talking, the better. In
other words, prayer is conversation with
God.

But praying should be more than just
words. Prayer is a deep expression of the
soul—an experience of real communication
with our Creator. It should involve living in
such a way that everything we do can
become an act of prayer.

Too often we hear people talk about
the sacred and the secular as though there
were some great difference between the
two. For the Christian there can be no
division. All he does should be considered

sacred, whether washing dishes, darning socks, digging ditches, singing in the sanctuary, watching a play, preaching in the pulpit, talking with a neighbor, saying a prayer or anything else. All should be sacred and, in effect, *an act of praying.* Praying is not only talking to God, or with Him, it is also an attitude—a style of life.

Praying Is Talking to God

When you are praying you are speaking to God. You speak not to another man, not to a special man, not to the best man—but to the Triune God!

A helpful definition of the Trinity, which has been passed from generation to generation, says:

"God is one essence or completeness, eternally existing in three persons: God the Father, God the Son, and God the Holy Spirit."

God is the Father; God is the Son; God is the Holy Spirit. God is all three. There is obviously a mystery here and our knowledge and understanding is certainly incomplete. Even a little understanding helps us to know that in our praying we can and should speak individually to the three persons of the Trinity, or to the Triune God Himself.

For example, we pray to God the Father in the Lord's Prayer: "Our Father who art in heaven" (Matt. 6:9, *NASB*). When we pray to Christ to forgive us our sins, we speak to God the Son (see Acts 7:59,60). When we ask the Holy Spirit to fill us with His power and strength we are speaking to the third person of the Trinity (see Jude 20). But when we pray, "O God,

help me" we are speaking to all three
persons of the Godhead.

We may address ourselves to any one
of the three persons of the Trinity or to
God as the Trinity. We not only may, but
should, pray to the Father, to the Son, to
the Holy Spirit, as well as to the Godhead.

God knows our hearts and our praying
is heard even though we may be confused
or in doubt as to the "address" or One to
whom we speak. However, in your growing
Christian experience, you will begin to
understand the work of each person of the
Trinity and address yourself to that person.[1]

You will find praying more meaningful
as you become aware of the nature of the
God to whom you are speaking. The
different names used for God in the Bible
provide us with an understanding of His
nature.

The Bible was written in the Hebrew
and Greek languages. Let's consider some
of God's Hebrew names and see some
aspects of His nature as revealed in the Old
Testament. These names give us a
beginning understanding of God.[2]

ELOHIM. The name *Elohim* is first used in Genesis 1:1, "In the beginning Elohim created the heavens and the earth." This name for God means "God the strong and mighty One, the God of creation and nature, One who is feared."

EL SHADDAI. *El Shaddai* refers to God as possessing all power in heaven and on earth before whom all else bows. He is the source of all blessing and comfort.

YAHWEH. *Yahweh* means "the God of grace, the God who is dependable, the faithful One, the God who is constant and in whom there is no change, the One who can be counted on to be all that He claims to be." Psalm 23 begins with the words, "Yahweh is my shepherd."

Praying Is Listening as God Talks with You

Praying is more than you talking to God. Praying is also *listening,* as God talks with you.

How does God communicate with you?

Primarily, He speaks through the Holy Scriptures. There can be no meaningful praying if there is no reading of the Holy Scriptures. This is very important, because a key goal for praying should be discerning God's will and direction. His Word, the Holy Scriptures, is the basic guide to understanding His will, for all believers.

God also speaks through His *Holy Spirit*. This is difficult to explain, yet it's real. You may feel led to a certain conclusion about a situation; or, for no reason, think of something long forgotten but needed at that time. There may come a sense of the presence of the Holy Spirit filling your soul, giving peace about a certain problem, or you may experience a flood of joy. He may quicken your conscience or concern about a certain situation or give you no peace until you act on a certain thing. God does speak to His people through His Holy Spirit. It is a wise person who takes the time to be silent long enough to let God speak and to listen when He does.

There should be times when you relax

completely, put everything out of your mind and allow God to speak. This is a time for re-creation—for renewal. To pour out your heart to God *is* important; but let God pour Himself into you!

You can do this listening, this "absorbing from God," at the beginning, in the middle, or at the end of your praying. You may even do it at times you have not specifically set aside for prayer. The important thing is to let God speak to you—from His Word and through His Spirit—in the quietness of your own soul. He will.

Praying Is the Way to Let God Work in Your Life

Out of a sense of futility, frustration or discouragement, some believers sometimes ask, "Why pray?" Praying can be the most important and most powerful activity in your entire life. Here are some reasons why:

1. *Praying does something for you personally.* Peace of mind, for example, can come through prayer.[3]

2. *Praying involves fellowship and communication with the Lord of the universe.* It helps you view life from a broader perspective and see the issues involved more clearly as you consider eternity.

3. *Praying is a key way to grasp the will of God.* Once you know God's will you can surrender to His leading and direction. As you surrender to God's will, you receive not only peace but feelings of power, direction, and accomplishment.

4. *Praying is you talking to God and God talking to you.* These points have been made already, but they bear repeating. You can't have a meaningful relationship with anyone unless you communicate, and that communication has to go both ways, between the two of you.

5. *God hears and answers our prayers.* Scripture promises that "everyone who asks receives; and he who seeks finds; and to him who knocks it shall be opened" (Luke 11:10, *NASB*).

Do you really need any more reasons for praying than these?

Praying Is Telling God, "So Let It Be!"

Amen is the word we use to close most of our prayers. But why? Amen is more than a nice way to let the people know you are at the end of your prayer.

Amen is really a scriptural word of affirmation in the belief that God has heard our prayer and is more desirous of answering our prayer than we can feel in our heart that we have need of these requests.

Amen is a statement of faith in the power of God to answer our prayer. Amen is a submitting of our will to Him with a "So let it be!"

In the next chapter you begin your study of Praise, the first of five essential facets of prayer. As you do so, it is our prayer that God will be at work in you "giving you the will and the power to achieve his purpose" (Phil. 2:13, *Phillips*).

Amen! So let it be!

CHAPTER TWO

Praise

"Praise the Lord!"

What is praise? To praise means "to speak well of." It means "to bless." It means "to enter into joyfully," as in a hymn sung from the depths of the soul. Praise means to shout, to extol, to honor God.

How do we praise God? To begin with, let's look at two Hebrew words found in the Bible, which are translated into English as "praise."

**Real Praise Requires
Total Involvement**
HALLELU. One of the words most

frequently used in the praise of God in the Old Testament is the Hebrew word *hallelu,* from which we get our English word "hallelujah." For example, Psalm 111 states, "I will praise *[hallelu]* the Lord with my whole heart. . . . His praise *[hallelu]* endureth forever" (see verses 1,10, *KJV*). Other passages of Scripture use this word of praise with singing or music, which involves the concept of *praise with one's total being.*

Have you ever heard the "Hallelujah Chorus" from Handel's *Messiah*? It's a song of praise to God. A choir can never sing this masterpiece halfheartedly and do it justice. To be sung properly, the "Hallelujah Chorus" demands a choir's total involvement. Watch the choir members as they sing it. If they are good musicians, they will put their whole being into the singing of this great work.

Traditionally, the majesty of the "Hallelujah Chorus" calls for the audience to stand while it is sung. So great is this work of praise that it requires involvement by listeners as well as those presenting it.

This total involvement—on the part of choir and audience—gives a hint of what is meant by "praise" when we think of the word *hallelu.*

BARACHA. Another key Hebrew word for praise is the word *baracha* which means "to bless or adore."[4] We read of offering adoration—*baracha*—to God. This is a form of praise. Glorifying or praising God is a real part of its meaning.

The word *baracha* is used in connection with a blessing given on bended knees. At the heart of the word *baracha* is the Hebrew concept that everything belongs to God. Psalm 24:1 states, "The earth is the Lord's, and the fulness thereof; the world, and they that dwell therein" (*KJV*). Since all belongs to God, nothing should be taken without a *baracha* or blessing. Hebrew tradition says that "if one fails to offer a blessing or *baracha* as he takes from life, he is robbing God."

It is the wise person who offers a *baracha* for every part of life: as thanksgiving or blessing before or after meals, for a new car, picking up a pay check, enjoying the beauty of a sunset, smelling a flower, breathing spring air, tasting fresh bread, watching a child play—for absolutely everything! All should be received with praise, blessing, adoration and thanksgiving.

Too many prayers consist of begging, asking or demanding from God, as if the world were our own private possession and He owed us what we are asking. The church often sings the hymn, "This is my father's world, God is the ruler yet." If we believe this, we should ask of God humbly and receive from Him with grateful hearts, full of praise for the creator and ruler of the universe. Because God is who He is, our praying should always include praise and blessing toward Him. Praising God is primary. It should be a regular part of daily communication with Him.

It Helps to Praise When the Going Gets Tough

HYMNOS. The New Testament adds Greek words to the Hebrew words, giving

us broader meanings of praise. One
significant Greek word used to praise God
is *hymnos* from which we get our English
word "hymn." Acts 16:25 tells of Paul and
Silas in the dark, damp, smelly Philippian
prison. At midnight they "prayed, and sang
praises unto God." The Greek word
hymnos is translated as "sang praise to
God." When the going got tough, these
men prayed and sang praises to God. It
was a form of worship. There was no
mention of "Woe is me," "Why did this
happen to me?" or "God, where are you?"
Instead, there was praying and singing of
praise.

Job also had hard times and problems.
His flocks were killed, his servants
murdered; then his sons and daughters died
in a "great wind." He was reduced to
nothing. Total heartache and financial ruin
were his. What did Job do? Complain? No!
Did he beg God to deliver him? No! Did he
lose faith in God? No! He had all the hurts,
but he still held on to God.

Scripture says Job "arose and tore his
robe and shaved his head," (symbolizing

grief) "and he fell to the ground and *worshiped*." Then he said, "Naked I came from my mother's womb, and naked I shall return there. The Lord gave and the Lord has taken away. Blessed *(baracha)* be the name of the Lord" (see Job 1:20,21, *NASB*).

Here is a profound lesson in facing tragedy, problems and hard times. Rather than complaining, you worship. Worship includes praise. You cannot worship without praise. "Blessed (*baracha*) be the name of the Lord." In praise, *baracha, hallelu, hymnos,* you lift your soul above the circumstance to the reality that God is in control of even that situation.

The positive practical results of praise in times of trouble can be very real and personal. Not long ago, one of the saints of our church was deathly ill. Each member of the family shared in the suffering of their loved one. It was difficult and death was sure to come soon. One of the church elders, a man of prayer, met with the family and prayed. His prayer consisted almost totally of praise, adoration and thanksgiving to God. He recounted the blessing of God in the past, and even gave praise to God for the present. The effect was immediate. The spirit of that family was lifted by that prayer of praise!

This does not mean that you ignore tragedy and suffering. Instead, it means that you lift your eyes above the tragedy to the One who knows the end from the beginning, to the One who made this world and all that is in it.

Are you facing a tragedy, problems or hard times? Try praising God in your situation. Praise God on behalf of the friend who is hurting, or the pain you are experiencing. Praising God reminds you that He is in charge, that He loves His children in any and all circumstances.

How to Make Praise Part of Your Life-Style

Psalm 111 speaks of praising God with your whole heart, in the company of the upright (v. 1). Psalm 111 also promises that praise is a lasting work and will not vanish. "His praise endureth forever" (v. 10). We

need a total, life-long attitude of praise.
Praising can and needs to become a natural
part of all we do. It's an important part of
our fellowship with God. Everything you do
all day long, whether it's working in the
office, studying, puttering around the
house, playing with the children or
worshiping in the sanctuary, can be done to
the praise of God.

Psalm 112 promises blessings to the
person who praises God by delighting in
His commandments and being obedient to
them. This Psalm promises inner strength
and steadfastness to the one who adopts a
life-style of praise and obedience to God.

Psalm 113:3 *(TLB)* advises us to
"praise him from sunrise to sunset!" Psalm
146:1,2 *(TLB)* adds, "Praise the Lord! Yes,
really praise him! I will praise him as long
as I live, yes, even with my dying breath."
Praising the Lord should be and can be our
continuous attitude toward life.

Psalm 147 gives a simple but profound
reason for praising the Lord: *it is good.* The
Lord is great. It is good that we praise Him
always!

Try memorizing psalms of praise, as well as other passages of Scripture. These can help you put into words the praise you feel in your own soul.

Go Ahead . . . Praise the Lord!

Praising God is not just sitting quietly, meekly, weakly, in a corner. It is singing, shouting, dancing, speaking well of. It is putting your whole being into an avalanche of adoration. The word "praise" is used over 250 times in the Scriptures. "Praise the Lord in thanksgiving"; "Praise the Lord in confession"; "Praise the Lord in blessing"; "Praise the Lord in giving": "Praise the Lord in stretching out the hand"; "Praise the Lord in speaking well."

Go ahead and praise the Lord! *Hallelu, baracha, hymnos.* Sing a hymn of praise. But let your praise be more than words. Show praise in your living. Use the *baracha* to appreciate all that is about you. Look at a flower. *Baracha!* Pronounce a *baracha* over your home and food and family and friends and church.

And use the *hallelu* to praise God with

your total being. Sing a hymn. Repeat a
Psalm. Stand up and dance. Blow a
trumpet. Think on the greatness of God.
Go ahead. Praise Him! He is still our
eternal God. *Hallelu!*

Personal Response . . . Praise

(This book is designed for you to write
in. Please do! You may also want to use
your own paper for additional notes.)

1. Read Isaiah 52:7-10. Then take a
few minutes to relax. Have you stopped

lately to smell a flower, look at the beauty
of a piece of wood, listen to a bird, breathe
of the fresh air, or watch a child at play?
Do it now, and allow your heart to fill with
praise, blessing, and adoration to God.
Look carefully around you right now. List
at least six things or reasons that prompt
you to praise the Lord:

2. Read Psalm 150 at least five times. If
you are alone, you may want to do what
David did (see 2 Sam. 6:14). Dance before
God! Stand up, use your head, hands,
arms, and legs like a graceful ballet dancer,
orchestra conductor, or soaring bird. (If you
have a praise hymn on a record or tape this
can help you in expressing your praise.)
Use your entire body to praise God! It may
seem awkward to you at first, but
concentrate your thoughts totally on Him,
not yourself. You may experience a new

joy in praising God! You may just want to raise your hands to Him in praise to signify your open heart and mind before the Lord.

3. Read your favorite Psalm. Take time to memorize it, so that you can recite it as your praise to God. Many times in the future you'll be able to praise God using the memory of this Psalm. (If you haven't a favorite, read Psalms 147, 148, 149 and 150.)

4. Read Psalm 149:1-4 as you consider new ways to praise God. Do you play an instrument? Use it to play a song or hymn of praise to God. It doesn't have to be "concert perfect." Play (or just sing) it for His hearing only. He may bring new music or words to you. If so, write them down:

5. Are there any of your circumstances which seem to you like a prison? Read about Paul's and Silas' prison circumstances in Acts 16:19-34. List some of your circumstances below. Then list some reasons for praise. Start right this minute honestly praising God for every one of your circumstances. Begin worshiping Him for all that He is and has done for you. Experience the liberating joy that Paul and Silas experienced in the Philippian prison, worshiping God in the middle of imprisoning circumstances.

My circumstances   *My praise*

6. Make a list of your friends. Praise God for giving them to you. Can you understand the reasoning for doing so as you read and consider Romans 12:1-21?

My friends   *Notes of praise on Romans 12*
_____   _____

7. Is there someone with whom you are upset? Listen to the "still small voice" of God as you read Romans 12:14-21; 13:8-10; and 1 John 2:7-11. Right now, stop and ask God to forgive you. Praise Him for bringing that person into your life. Ask Him to replace your hurt, bitterness, or resentment with His love and praise.

                 I will still praise God
I am upset with: *because:*
_____   _____

8. Do you know someone in a retirement home? Read James 1:27 and Matthew 25:31-46; then go to the home and praise God with them. Help them praise Him to the very end of life.

9. Meditate on Romans 5:1-5 and Romans 15:1-6 in your favorite version. Now thoughtfully consider the following: Do you have friends who are going through some "deep waters" at this time? Ask God if He would have you go and pray with them. When you get there, thank God for all of His goodness, and watch their spirits lift as they remember how good God really is!

10. Do you have a consistently praising spirit? Are you naturally positive and always praising God? For a healthy pattern to follow, read 1 Thessalonians 5:12-28 and 1 John 5:1-5. God would like to give *you* a spirit of praise in everything *you* do. Ask Him! Praise the Lord and He will continue to show you new ways to praise Him.

Notes on new ways I can praise God

_____

11. Consider Philippians 4:4-9 and then answer these questions: What are you going to do differently? What do you understand more clearly, as a result of reading and experiencing this chapter on praise?

For additional ideas on developing personal praise, see Chapter 7 "Your Praying Notebook: A Tool to Revolutionize Your Prayer Life," Section 1 on Praise.

CHAPTER THREE

Confession

"I confess."

These are almost always two extremely difficult words to say. But confession is the vital step . . . it is the only action we can take that results in forgiveness and the freedom of a clear conscience. The benefits far outweigh the costs.

There are two parts to confession. The first part of confession is *profession*. "Thou art the Christ, the Son of the living God" (Matt. 16:16). The other part of confession is an *admission* of our sins and asking forgiveness. Complete confession includes both profession and admission.

Unconfessed sin harbored in our lives is sometimes the reason for unanswered prayer (see Ps. 66:18). Unconfessed sin keeps us from God while confession brings us to Him.

Confession Starts with Profession

The starting point of confession—true confession—is to confess/profess Jesus to be God. This confession cannot be mere words. It must be the result of a deep conviction that He is our only source of eternal hope and salvation. At the heart of this kind of confession is the idea that we cannot make it on our own. As humans we can do absolutely nothing to save our own souls. We are entirely and absolutely dependent on Him.

The best of our good deeds falls embarrassingly short of God's standards. We are constantly in need of His forgiveness, so we confess that we need Jesus Christ and profess to have received Him. With this confession He becomes our

Lord and Saviour and we His people. This is primary. If we have not made this profession, our praying will be mostly meaningless. But when we do make this honest, personal profession, God takes control of our life and destiny. We commit our lives to Him and follow the Lordship of Jesus Christ. We go where He wants us to go and do what He wants us to do.

Jesus promised, "And whatsoever ye shall ask in my name, that will I do, that the Father may be glorified in the Son. If ye shall ask any thing in my name, I will do it" (John 14:13,14, *KJV*). There is more to this promise than just praying the words, "in Jesus' name." The *core* of the promise is the fact that when we pray in His name we confess our belief in the fact that Jesus is the Lord and He can, and will, do what we are asking if it is His will.

Profession includes committing your will to the will of God, putting God in control of your life and destiny. As Christians we follow the commands of Jesus Christ as revealed in the Holy Scriptures under the leading of the Holy Spirit.

It's important to remember that we can count on the fact that God will not lead us in ways that are contrary to the teachings of the Holy Scripture.

Someone knocked at our door one night. When we opened the door, there stood a man in his late thirties. He came in and, as we talked, he told me his wife had asked him to leave. Apparently she was "very spiritual." After prayer she felt that the Holy Spirit had revealed to her that she and her husband should no longer stay together because she had other work to do. However, the Holy Spirit does not suddenly say, "Get rid of your husband." There must have been some other means of accomplishing her new work than dissolving the marriage.

Have you read newspaper accounts of people claiming they were acting under God's orders to murder someone or to commit some other horrible deed? God does not issue such orders. The person who makes such a claim is spiritually and psychologically unbalanced and needs professional help.

Sometimes people blame God for these actions or excuse themselves by trying to say God has commanded them. God, however, is not to blame. Responsibility rests with the person concerned, who is, in fact, trying to use God to serve his own purposes rather than discovering God's laws and God's will, and becoming obedient to them.

A very basic part of profession is that we totally surrender to the will of God and become willing to obey Him. Surrendering to God's will is an essential step towards victorious living.

Our son became interested in rocketry. He bought the equipment and began assembling the kit. A brass contact part was missing. He couldn't replace that with paper or wood; he had to have a specially designed piece of brass. So he had to go back and get the right part. He had to *surrender* to the demand of the launcher by getting what was required before he could complete his project.

Our other son has a great interest in model railroading. Before the model trains will run he has to turn on the current, the track has to be clean and the connections firm. He has to *surrender* to the laws of electrical current.

I've tried to play golf. I had to *surrender* my free will to the demands of the laws of the game of golf. I can't play effective golf with a baseball bat. I have to use the right clubs. I have to stand by the ball in a certain way. I have to grip the club just right. I have to swing the club in just the proper way and I have to keep my eye on the ball. If I do all of these things correctly I have surrendered to the laws of golf, and I am able to hit the ball where I want and have a better chance for a good score.

By surrendering to the will of God and His commandments we begin to really live; but surrendering means that *He must be Lord of all our life.* The Scriptures help us know the will of God. They give us the only eternally true and consistent correction and direction in our lives. The Bible becomes our rule book so that we can walk wisely and run confidently after the pattern that Jesus set for us.

To say it another way, as wise Christians we will take the time to study the Scriptures carefully and surrender to God's will as we discover it, so that we will grow in the faith, understanding and doing the will of God.

But why surrender?

We surrender to Christ because of His love. The basis of this surrender to God isn't His stronger power or a "bigger stick." The core of Christian living is love. Jesus said that the greatest command is to love God, love your neighbor and love yourself (see Matt. 22:37-39). We make a profession based on this love. It is because of the love of God that we have life (John 3:16). This truth we profess to be our only hope for eternal life, and the basis for our prayers of confession.

Confession Means Admitting, "I Have Sinned"

We become Christians by believing that Jesus is the Son of God and the only Saviour of mankind. But we must also confess/admit *to God* that we have sinned and are sinners (Rom. 3:23), recognize that Christ died on the cross for our sins (1 Pet. 2:24), and invite Him into our lives to become Lord of our lives (Rev. 3:20).

Life often is a struggle. Even a Christian's life is a struggle. It is a struggle against sin, compromise, pride—the list is practically endless. We look at ourselves and often feel like crying with the apostle Paul, "Wretched man that I am!" (Rom. 7:24, *KJV*).

Has the Holy Spirit put His finger on some area of your life that needs to be made right? Maybe you have spoken harshly. You may have, with all good intentions, borrowed some money but have not paid it back as you promised. Have you communicated gossip, hurting someone's good name? Have you taken advantage of someone in a way that would be embarrassing to you if it were made public? Have you determined to "never forgive" someone? The list of possibilities goes on and on.

Whatever the sin, the first step is admission/confession *to God.* Ask His

forgiveness first (1 John 1:9). This step can
be difficult, but the next one is often even
harder. In some cases, perhaps confession
needs to be made *to the person you have
wronged*.

Your ego may argue, "But my friends
will think I'm strange. They can destroy me.
They can ruin my reputation, take my job,
take me to court."

It's difficult to make things right with
someone you have offended. It's
humiliating. It hurts the pride. You may
look desperately for some way to avoid this
personal confession. But the truth is, there
is no way.

If you want spiritual victory, you must
face the problem. Make your confession. If
necessary return something, take back a
remark, pay a debt, etc. It may be painful,
awkward, embarrassing, but it's the way to
regain a clean clear conscience.

A clear conscience is one of the most
valued possessions anyone, anywhere, can
have. Let the chips fall where they may,
God doesn't abandon us. If we confess our
sins, says Scripture, *God* is faithful. He

forgives even when others might not.
Victory sometimes comes very hard. But in
this victory there is strengthened character
and renewed faith. The doors of
communication with God and our friends
spring open. Love is regained, and the
freshness of forgiveness relieves your soul
from guilt. You no longer need to avoid the
eyes of the one you have wronged.

It's always humiliating to take the step
of personal confession. It is risky. But it is
worth all the risk. When confession is
made, we really begin growing spiritually.
Meaningful praying is once again available
to us.

God Forgives . . . and Forgets!
When we honestly confess our sins,
God forgives us. We have His word on it:
"If we freely admit that we have sinned, we
find God utterly reliable and
straightforward—he forgives our sins and
makes us thoroughly clean" (1 John 1:9,
Phillips).

In 1 John 1:9 the word for forgive
comes from the Greek word, *aphieemi*.

Seeing how this word is used in different contexts in the New Testament helps define it. For example, Jesus went in the village of Capernaum, found Peter's mother-in-law sick with fever and touched her. Scripture says the fever "left" her (Matt. 8:15). The Greek word *aphieemi* is used for the word "left." Matthew 4:20 reports that the disciples left their nets and followed Him. Again, the word *aphieemi* is used for "left."

To be forgiven, then, means that our sins have left us . . . they are gone. We are no longer under the guilt or the condemnation. The sins are gone and there is no more need for confession of these sins. They are gone; they are forgiven.

If you have sincerely made a confession of a certain sin, then do *not* continually repeat the confession of that sin. First John 1:9 says that if you have confessed a sin, it is forgiven. Forgiveness literally means that particular sin has left you. It means it is taken away and you start anew.

Accept His forgiveness and go on from there. Be careful, however, not to take advantage of God. Don't commit the same sin willfully or carelessly, thinking, "God will forgive." If you do, your prayers of confession will stick in your throat because you will know they are not genuine.

**God Forgives,
but Scars Remain**

It is important to understand a key point: You can be forgiven by God for sins; you can be forgiven by others and you can forgive others; forgiveness is available; but there are certain marks of sin that cannot be erased.

A close friend of ours was an alcoholic. He has been forgiven, cleansed and sober for five years. But he still carries the scars of alcoholism; he may die of cirrhosis of the liver.

There are many other examples. People get involved in an adulterous relationship. The scars and memories follow them the rest of their lives. They can be completely forgiven by God. He "forgets," but they will never be able to forget.

You can take a piece of wood and drive nails into it. Then pull out the nails and put putty in the holes. Sand down the wood, polish it, make it beautiful. You can even use it in a piece of expensive furniture, but it will *always carry scars of those nails.*

Confession and forgiveness of sins will pull the nails out of our lives. The Holy Spirit can cleanse, polish and make us beautiful, but the scars of that sin will always be there. Sin often leaves painful consequences and we must live with those scars for life.

What About Forgiving Others?

Jesus talked a lot about forgiveness and preached the need for reconciliation. We need to be willing to forgive someone as many times as that person comes and asks for our forgiveness (see Matt. 18:21,22).

A young mother was very troubled over her husband who was an alcoholic. When he was sober, he would apologize for getting drunk and beg forgiveness, but then he would go out and do the same thing again. He would come home in a drunken rage and beat her. He would then sleep off the drunkenness, sober up, beg forgiveness and promise not to do it again. But he did.

When she finally separated from her husband he begged her to come back, but she said no. Later he committed suicide and she is now haunted by the idea that she could have prevented his suicide if she had taken him back. She feels very guilty about his death.

She was willing to forgive him, and did forgive him, even though there were hurts and many bad memories. She was wise in that, when she realized that she and the children were being subjected to continued danger, she took the steps necessary to protect herself and the children. She tried to get her husband to accept professional help but he refused. He thought he could handle it himself, although he evidently couldn't. He made his own decisions and had to take full responsibility for them. Therefore, she should not feel guilty for his death. She did not cause it, he did.

We must be willing to forgive a person; but that does *not* mean we have to submit ourselves to continued abuse or danger by a person who makes a mockery of forgiveness. There are some people who not only need forgiveness, but also the professional help of a minister, doctor or counselor. The best thing we can do for the people with this kind of need is to take the risk of helping them to get professional care.

A businessman was timidly approached by one of his trusted employees who admitted stealing money from the company. The employee asked forgiveness. He was forgiven and began to repay the money. However, the businessman felt it would be unwise to put him back in the same position facing the same temptation.

To forgive others does not mean to become foolish; yet we are to forgive *completely*. There is no contradiction here, for confession and forgiveness should always include help and healing for the person who did the wrong.

Personal Response . . . Confession

1. Have you stopped to realize and profess to God and others that you can't make it to heaven on your own? See John

3:3, Ephesians 2:8,9 and Romans 6:23. Are you ready to profess your dependence on Him right now? If so, write a short prayer of profession/confession below:

2. Study Psalm 51. What is keeping you from being a totally clean vessel that God can use? What would you like to confess/admit to God and have Him forgive and forget forever? Quietly listen to God for five minutes, listing those things He brings to your mind that you need to confess to Him, and possibly confess to others. Will you trade these for a clear conscience right now?

Lord, forgive me for:

_____

3. Meditate on Matthew 6:14,15 and 5:23,24. Now list the ways people have "wronged you." They should ask your forgiveness, but forgive them first, even before they ask, and you will experience God's joy.

Lord, help me forgive:

_____

4. Carefully read Romans 3:21-26 and Philippians 4:4-20. Do you feel inferior and resent God for making you as you are? If so, admit this to Him and ask His forgiveness for your ungratefulness for all He has given you.

5. Consider Philippians 1:6, Ephesians 4:11-16 and 5:1-20. What kind of a person do you feel God wants you to be spiritually? Are you ready to ask Him to help you be that person? Ask Him now. Write down what He tells you:

6. What task(s) is there that no one else can do or wants to do that God has in mind for you to do, even though it may hurt your pride a little? Ask the Holy Spirit to enlighten you as you read Philippians 2:12-18.

Unimportant (or unpleasant) tasks God may want me to do:

7. Get alone in a quiet place. Read Psalm 66:18 and 1 John 1:9. How many people can you think of in the next five minutes of praying that you have wronged, resented, gossiped about, offended, or

maybe even hated, and have not asked God's forgiveness, or theirs? List them here:

Are you ready now to risk hurting your pride for eternal peace? If so, follow the next four steps:

   a. Realizing how easy it is to delay asking someone's forgiveness, set a time limit within which you will do it.
   b. Which person on the list is the hardest for you to ask forgiveness? Ask that one first, the others will be easier.
   c. If some have passed away, ask God to forgive you and to show you how He would have you "make things right."
   d. Cross the names off the list one at a time. Experience God's freedom, joy, clear conscience, and exciting life of sins forgiven.

8. See 1 John 1:9 and Matthew 5:23,24. Have you committed some crime for which you may have to face court, trial, and imprisonment? Ask God to forgive you, then ask your pastor or a Christian friend to go through these "deep waters" with you.

Remember that the scars of sin will constantly be with you, but you can still be a "beautiful piece of wood" with God's healing.

9. What are you going to do differently? What do you understand more clearly as a result of reading and doing what this chapter says? Read and memorize Proverbs 3:5,6.

For more help in personal confession, turn to Chapter 7: "Your Praying Notebook: A Tool to Revolutionize Your Prayer Life," especially Sections 2 and 3.

CHAPTER FOUR

Thanksgiving

"Thank you!"

Thanksgiving is simply expressing appreciation. It's an expression of personal humility and a giving of honor. When you can sincerely express thanks, you are more aware of God's greatness. You are living with a proper appreciation for all you have received from God.

There are three focuses for your thanksgiving. First, thank God for all He is and has done. Second, be thankful to God for others and for what He has done in their lives. Third, be thankful in every circumstance in your life.

**Thank God for All
He Is and Has Done**

What God really wants from you is your
thanksgiving: "What I want from you is
your true thanks; I want your promises
fulfilled. I want you to trust me in your
times of trouble, so I can rescue you, and
you can give me glory" (Ps. 50:14,15,
TLB).

God wants you to be aware of your
dependence on Him, aware of His
magnitude and majesty, aware of the good
things He gives you. Undoubtedly, you
want to give God the thanksgiving He
expects. But how? How can you develop
an attitude of thankfulness for what He is
and has done? There are at least three
ways:

You can magnify God in meditation. In
Psalm 69:30 David says, "I . . . will magnify
him with thanksgiving" *(KJV)*.

Have you ever taken a magnifying glass
to the beach? The beach is a different place
under a magnifying glass. Each individual
bit of sand becomes a little rock with
distinctive shapes and colors. The whole

magnified world comes more alive as we watch an ant cross the sand or find a piece of broken shell with its rainbow of colors. When you look at anything with a magnifying glass, you don't in fact make *it* larger. What happens is that *your image* of it becomes larger and clearer.

You can "magnify God" through meditating on His characteristics—His love, His understanding, His compassion, plus many others that come to mind. Any of these characteristics is reason enough to thank God, and as you meditate you become increasingly aware of and grateful for His greatness, His vastness and His love.

The psalmist says, "I will meditate on all Thy work, and muse on Thy deeds" (Ps. 77:12, *NASB*). God is so great, God is so wonderful, that soon your whole spirit is overflowing with thanksgiving!

You can thank God through singing praises to Him. In Psalm 95:2-7 David invites you to sing like this: "Come before him with thankful hearts. Let us sing him psalms of praise. For the Lord is a great

God, the great King of all gods. He controls the formation of the depths of the earth and the mightiest mountains; all are his. He made the sea and formed the land; they too are his. Come, kneel before the Lord our Maker, for he is our God. We are his sheep and he is our Shepherd. Oh, that you would hear him calling you today and come to him!" *(TLB).*

As you sit alone, or in a group, and meditate on God, sing your favorite song of thanksgiving. You don't need a great voice; perhaps you are a monotone. God does not care. Sing out with gladness and joy. Let your whole being give thanksgiving to God!

You can thank God by the giving of what you have and who you are. Scripture teaches that we are to bring tithes and offerings to the Lord. (See, for example, Mal. 3:10 and 1 Cor. 9:6-15.) As an act of thanksgiving, are you faithfully giving substantial and sacrificial gifts for the cause of Christ? Giving is most meaningful when you give out of love, as an expression of thanksgiving for all that God has given you.

That's precisely what Paul talks about in 2 Corinthians when he writes:

"Now this I say, he who sows sparingly shall also reap sparingly; and he who sows bountifully shall also reap bountifully. Let each one do just as he has purposed in his heart; not grudgingly or under compulsion; for God loves a cheerful giver. And God is able to make all grace abound to you, that always having all sufficiency in everything, you may have an abundance for every good deed; as it is written, 'He scattered abroad, he gave to the poor, His righteousness abides forever.'

"Now He who supplies seed to the sower and bread for food, will supply and multiply your seed for sowing and increase the harvest of your righteousness; you will be enriched in everything for all liberality, which through us is producing thanksgiving to God.

"For the ministry of this service is not only fully supplying the needs of the saints, but is also overflowing through many thanksgivings to God. Because of the proof given by this ministry they will glorify God for your obedience to your confession of the gospel of Christ, and for the liberality of your contribution to them and to all, while they also, by prayer on your behalf, yearn for you because of the surpassing grace of God in you. Thanks be to God for His indescribable gift!" (2 Cor. 9:6-15, *NASB*).

Giving to God from your bank account or your possessions is a practical way to show your thanksgiving. But gifts to God don't have to cost money to be precious. Consider, for example, giving God your impatience, your temper, your lustful thoughts, your pride, your craving for food. Along with your faults and weaknesses, give God your talents, gifts and strengths for His use, to His glory. That's what Paul is saying in two of Scripture's best known and most quoted verses:

"And so, dear brothers, I plead with you to give your bodies to God. Let them be a living sacrifice, holy—the kind he can accept. When you think of what he has done for you, is this too much to ask? Don't copy the behavior and customs of this world, but be a new and different person with a fresh newness in all you do and think. Then you will learn from your own experience how his ways will really satisfy you" (Rom. 12:1,2, *TLB*).

God wants all of you—the good and the not so good. He desires that you sacrifice yourself as a "gift"—to Him—by living out His salvation with thanksgiving.

Thanksgiving is more than putting money in offering plates. It is more than singing or talking. It is more than meditating. Thanksgiving is *living*. It includes helping others, loving others, sharing with others, being a person of integrity . . . the list is long.

Thanksgiving is living with an attitude of being so grateful to God that you express your gratitude in *all* of your life.

Thank God for What He Is Doing for Others

Giving thanks to God for being God and for His gifts and goodness to us is something you may do quite naturally. But do you ever stop to thank God for other people—*and what He has given them?* If you have to admit you rarely get around to thanking God on behalf of others, you aren't unique. A lot of people are in the same boat. But why?

One reason is that we just don't think about it. We have our own interests and concerns. Or, it may be we don't want to give God thanks for other people's success because we're jealous of it.

In Romans 1:8-10 the apostle Paul thanks God for the fact that his friends are growing in Jesus:

"First, I thank my God through Jesus Christ for all of you, because your faith is being reported all over the world. God, whom I serve with my whole heart in preaching the gospel of his Son, is my witness how constantly I remember you in my prayers at all times" *(NIV)*.

Paul wasn't jealous of the Christians at Rome. Their reputations as spiritual leaders were growing, and he was thankful to God.

It's easy to tell how much you actually love someone by whether or not you are thankful to God on their behalf when they are doing well.

For whom will you give God thanks for His goodness *to them?*

Thank God in Every Circumstance of Your Life

The Bible tells us we are to thank God in everything:

"Do not be anxious about anything, but in everything, by prayer and petition, with thanksgiving, present your requests to God. And the peace of God, which transcends all understanding, will guard your hearts and your minds in Christ Jesus" (Phil. 4:6,7, *NIV*).

Don't worry? Give thanks *in everything?* That's right!

Did you know that it's an absolute impossibility to resent something for which you are honestly thankful? You just can't do it! What is there in your life that you deeply resent? Honestly thank God for that situation or that person. Feel God give you His peace of mind. "Be joyful always; pray continually; give thanks in all circumstances, for this is God's will for you in Christ Jesus" (1 Thess. 5:16-18, *NIV*).

Whatever your circumstances are, give God thanks for them. It's His will for you today. You may have problems, but God uses problems to bring you to full maturity in faith. Give Him thanks!

Personal Response. . .
Thanksgiving

1. Psalm 136:1 says, "O give thanks unto the Lord; for he is good: for his mercy endureth for ever" *(KJV)*. List as many of God's qualities as you can. Meditate on each one of these qualities in thanksgiving for the next few minutes.

God's qualities   *My thanksgiving*
_____   _____

2. Study carefully 1 Peter 5:7 and Romans 5:3-5. Are you willing to give God what He really wants from you—a thankful heart for all He has done for you? List the major problems you've had in the past five years, and thank God for having brought you through them:

3. Follow David's command as found in Psalm 147:7. Write a song of thanksgiving or a poem to God right now. It doesn't have to be long or a masterpiece. If you aren't poetic just let what's in your heart flow onto the paper.

4. Study Romans 2:1-16; 1 Thessalonians 5:23; and Romans 6:1-23. What secret "personal sins" are you holding onto that God would be pleased to receive as a thanksgiving offering from you? List them here and give them to God—*now:*

5. Do you resent how someone is "getting ahead" in life? Instead, try thanking God for their success and growth. Read what Paul has to say in 1 Thessalonians 5:11-22. List at least six things you could do for others. Can you then add: "Thank you, Lord, for how you are blessing *(name)*."

6. Look at 2 Timothy 1:3-7. Who has been important in your spiritual maturity? Make a list of these friends, thanking God for them. Write them a note today telling them that God has brought them to mind while you were praying, and that they are very special to you for their influence in your life.

7. What are your big and small problems today? Make a list. Read 1 Peter

5:7. Begin thanking God for each one of them. Ask Him to help you begin looking for the lessons He has in mind for you to learn through each of your problems.

My problems   *What I'm learning*
_____   _____

    8. Who has wronged you? List them below. Thank God for that person(s) and for the experience of allowing you to grow because of that wrong. Consider Jesus' words in Matthew 5:38-48 and ask Him to take away your spirit of resentment and replace it with a spirit of true thanksgiving.

I feel I've been wronged by:
_____

Lord, help me to:
_____

9. For your personal devotions tonight, study 1 Timothy 6:6-10; Matthew 25:14-30; and Proverbs 31:10-31. List some important material possessions. Thank God for them, and ask for wisdom in their use.

10. Meditate on Romans 6:22,23; 12:1,2; and 1 Corinthians 4:1-5. Then make a list of the things you can do to make your life a living sacrifice of thanksgiving to God.

I will be a living sacrifice by:

For additional suggestions in learning how to offer
thanksgiving, see Chapter 7 "Your Praying Notebook: A Tool to
Revolutionize Your Prayer Life," Section 4.

CHAPTER FIVE

Petition

"Lord, help me!"

It's the championship game. The people in the stands are hoarse from cheering. The home team is behind. Four runs are needed to win. The bases are loaded. There are two outs and the coach sends in a sophomore pinch hitter who is a Christian. The boy walks up to the plate, puts the bat over his shoulder, and takes his stance. As the pitcher begins to wind up, the boy silently prays, "God, help me hit a home run."

A family man has been unemployed for three long humiliating months. It's been hard on the family. He walks into the office for a job interview. He prays, "God, help me to get this job."

A medical student is studying for final exams and prays, "God, help me to understand and remember this material."

A mother living in a drought-stricken country prays for food and rain so she and her family will not starve.

A young person wrestles with the decision about his life's vocation and prays, "God help me pick the job where I might do your will."

These are prayers of *petition*. To petition is to ask God for something for yourself, to bring your own special requests or concerns to Him.

Some sincere Christian believers say, "I never ask God on my own behalf. I always ask for the needs of others." This well-meaning statement shows an incorrect understanding of prayer. Scripture clearly teaches that God wants you to ask Him to meet *your* needs:

"You do not have because you do not ask" (Jas. 4:2, *NASB*).

"Ask and it will be given to you; seek and you will find; knock and the door will be opened to you. For everyone who asks receives; he who seeks finds; and to him who knocks, the door will be opened. Which of you, if his son asks for bread, will give him a stone? Or if he asks for a fish, will give him a snake? If you, then, though you are evil, know how to give good gifts to your children, how much more will your Father in heaven give good gifts to those who ask him! In everything, do to others what you would have them do to you, for this sums up the Law and the Prophets" (Matt. 7:7-12, *NIV*).

Honestly Ask for Whatever You Want

Never shy away from complete honesty in your petitioning (asking) of God. God is interested in you, and *you* are interested in you. Not asking God on your own behalf is like trying to give the impression that you aren't interested in yourself. That's dishonest! You are interested in yourself, and God knows it.

Ask for help in all areas of life. Ask God

about your talents, decisions, possessions, relations with other people, etc.

Jesus was completely honest with God when He was praying in the garden just before His crucifixion. In all honesty He asked, "My Father! If it is possible, let this cup be taken away from me" (Matt. 26:39, *TLB*).

Jesus apparently had some deep personal wants as He faced the cross—humanly wanting to live, to avoid rejection, to avoid the pain of crucifixion. But His perfectly mature petitioning attitude was "I want your will, not mine" (Matt. 26:39, *TLB*).

Ask God for whatever you honestly want and then just as honestly assure Him that you want His will rather than your own, even if it means not getting what you are asking for right now. This is basic to mature prayers of petition.

Why do you want what you want? Is it to get recognition for yourself or to bring glory and honor to God? Are you wanting God to become your tool to accomplish your desire? Or do you want Him to use you as His tool to accomplish His desires?

James told us: "You do not have, because you do not ask." In the very next verse he adds: "When you ask, you do not receive, because you ask with wrong motives, that you may spend what you get on your pleasures" (Jas. 4:3, *NIV*).

Within mature, honest petitioning there must also be the deep desire that God should receive the glory. "Whatever you do, do it all for the glory of God" (1 Cor. 10:31, *NIV*).

Honestly bring all of your needs and wishes to God, but within all of your petitions, your attitude should be, "I want your will, not my will. Bring glory to yourself and not to me." Then you'll know the satisfaction of having rightly communicated your petitions to God.

And what about those situations where you may try hard to have the right motive, but can't even determine your true motive. You may ask, "Is this prayer selfish?" Let God decide that. God is still God, and in His great wisdom He is still able to give you what is best for you even when you ask unwisely for the wrong things.

A couple of Halloweens ago, my children were out "trick or treating" and brought home large sacks of candy. My young son, then four, asked me if he could eat the whole bag that night. I appreciated the sincerity of his request, and it was a very honest one; but, of course, I had to say no. I try to give him only what's best for him. I help him grow by refusing certain of his requests, giving him what is best for him in the long run.

Be Persistent but Not Impatient

There is a big difference between patient persistence (persevering) in prayer, and impatient, self-centered demanding. When you "demand" you are like an impatient child. You ask God for what you want and then fret because He doesn't come through on time with your request.

If you impatiently demand of God, He may let you have what you want, though it isn't best for you. But when you've gotten what you want, motivated by self-centered impatience, you may experience a leanness within your soul—and that is *not* comfortable.

If you experience this "soul leanness" you may not feel like praying, but that's exactly what you *must* do! Confess your impatience and ask God's forgiveness. Recommit yourself to Him sincerely wanting only His will for your life. It won't take long for His peace and joy to flood your soul.

I Want Your Will, Lord, but What Is It?

Suppose you have asked God honestly for what you want. You have told Him you want His will rather than your own, and that He would receive the glory rather than yourself. And yet you are still left with the question, "What is God's will in this situation?"

God reveals His will in three specific ways: He has put the vast majority of the answers you need into the Holy Scriptures; He sometimes directs you through what some people call His "leading" or "guidance"; He sometimes reveals His will for you by working through other people to answer your petitions.

Let's look at these three concepts in more detail:

1. *You can determine God's will in many situations by consistently and prayerfully reading His word.* Always ask, as you are reading the Scriptures and praying about a particular situation, "Lord, what do the Scriptures show me to be your will in this situation?" These two cannot be separated. Your understanding of the Scriptures and your praying move along together.

You need consistent fellowship with God in reading the Scriptures so that the Holy Spirit can give you direction based on scriptural facts. If you have no knowledge of Scripture—what the will of God is for all of His people—it is extremely difficult, if not impossible, to determine God's will for yourself.

Studying Scripture to find God's will may seem like a slow process. But finding God's will is *not* something that usually happens overnight. It isn't like making an appointment with a counselor to have him

tell you what you want to know at four
o'clock next Tuesday.

Just as you mature physically and
emotionally, you seek to mature in your
praying. As you consistently, prayerfully
read the Scriptures, you become much
more sensitive to the true leading of God.

When seeking God's will it's usually
best to steer away from the hasty S.O.S.
approach. During emergencies, however,
you may need to use the S.O.S. kind of
praying. If you are facing an S.O.S.
situation today, counsel with a mature
Christian about this need—someone who
knows the Scriptures thoroughly and in
whose personal testimony of faith you have
complete confidence.

2. *You occasionally determine the will
of God through what some speak of as His
"leading or guidance," or the "leading of
the Holy Spirit."* You may have heard
pastors tell of being "led of the Lord" to
speak on a certain subject. They have
asked God His will and He has led them to
a specific topic. Some Christians say, "God
told me to do this." Many Christians speak

of this direct inner leading of the Lord as "guidance."

At times, God definitely impresses individual Christians to do or say a specific thing. There is one word of caution that I must add here. *All guidance is not from God.* "Guidance" can come from our own motives, dreams, and desires. "Guidance" can come from Satan. Counterfeit guidance can come from almost anywhere and seem to be guidance from the Lord.

All guidance must be verified by its agreement with the Holy Scriptures. In some cases you may want to seek the advice of another mature Christian to see if he agrees that your guidance is really from God.

If you feel led in a certain direction, and it agrees with the Scriptures, you have the assurance that you are moving in the right direction. However, if the "guidance" contradicts the Scriptures, beware; it's not God's leading.

3. *Sometimes you learn God's will as He has other Christians answer your secret prayer requests.* Several years ago some

dear friends of mine felt led of the Lord to go by faith to the mission field. They began asking the Lord to supply the money needed while serving Him as missionaries if it was His will that they go. In prayer they decided they would need $153 per month. My friends never asked their friends for a single penny, nor did they let their needs be known to anyone; but they did ask God for $153 per month.

They testify today that for years, documented by their income ledger, they received exactly $153 per month to the penny! The money came from different sources, never having the same combination of people giving. God led people to answer their petitions each month, assuring that they were in His will.

A word of caution here. You may pray secretly and ask God to move in much the same way these friends did, only to discover that the answer is not the same. Does this then mean that you must not do that thing about which you prayed? Not necessarily. God moves in different ways. He gives assurance in unique ways that are meaningful. God gives his verification in response to the "fleece" that we put out. (See the story of Gideon in Judg. 6:36-40.)

There may come times of difficulty and even opposition from sources you expect to be supportive. But you are still convinced by other means, such as Scripture or the presence of the Holy Spirit, that this is the will of God for you. Your faith is between you and your Lord. You must answer to Him for your life and the talents you have received. At times a door may seem closed; but God will not abandon you. He still leads as the Lord of your life. Follow Him!

100% His Will—0% Mine?

In your secret thoughts, you may ask, "Must I always have to ask for God's will to be done, for Him to get the glory? Isn't there anything that I can get just because I want it; because it's my will, and I want the glory?"

Seeking God's glory and will 100% of the time might seem dull, even oppressive, but right here you have found one of the most profound paradoxes of Christian

living. When you give up all rights to
yourself, and desperately want only His will
and His glory, He gives you the total,
complete, fully satisfied desires of your
heart.

The apostle Paul speaks of the plan of
God's glory in Romans 5:1,2: "Therefore
having been justified by faith, we have
peace with God through our Lord Jesus
Christ, through whom also we have
obtained our introduction by faith into this
grace in which we stand; and we exult in
hope of the glory of God" *(NASB)*.

Joy comes when you share in the glory
of God. That's the best. When you do the
will of God you give up your imperfect rule
for His sovereign rule. It's like having to
perform major surgery when all you have
for training is a brief course in first aid.
Instead of going ahead on your inadequate
own, you call in a skilled doctor to perform
the operation and do it right.

No longer do you stumble along hoping
you are on the right course. Instead there is
certainty in living, a feeling of confidence
and well-being.

One way to look at it, as a friend of mine says, "You give yourself to Him, and then *He gives you back to yourself,* enhanced and fulfilled. And when *that* happens you can truly rejoice in sharing the glory of God!"

Try it and see. You will find, time and time again, the truth and practical reality of David's insight in Psalm 37:4, "Be delighted with the Lord. Then he will give you all your heart's desires" *(TLB).*

Personal Response . . . Petition
1. Read Luke 6:38; Luke 11:5-13; Luke 22:42. Petition praying is asking, "God, if you have no other plans that are better for me than this, if you feel I need it, and it will bring you glory, please grant me this particular request."

a. Make a list of all the things you think you would really like.

b. Star the ten you would choose as most important to you.

c. Can you see any reasons why God may not give you these? (Is it His will as verified by Scripture? Do you really need it? Will it bring Him glory?)

d. Now circle the ones you honestly feel free to ask Him to give you.

2. Check your list above. Is there anything on that list you want so badly it causes you to resent God for not giving it to you? Are you ready to ask His forgiveness for putting *your* wants before *His* will?

Read the following poem, plus 1 Corinthians 3:1-4,10-21; Philippians 3:17—4:2; 2 Timothy 4:14-19.

I asked for strength that I might achieve;
  He made me weak that I might obey.
I asked for health that I might do greater things;
  I was given grace that I might do better things.
I asked for riches that I might be happy;
  I was given poverty that I might be wise.
I asked for power that I might have the praise of men;
  I was given weakness that I might feel the need of God.
I asked for all things that I might enjoy life;
  I was given life that I might enjoy all things.
I received nothing that I asked for, all that I hoped for,
  My prayer was answered.[5]

3. Does your life bring glory to God, or might God be ashamed of the way you are living? Confess this to Him, and ask Him to show you ways you can bring glory to Him through your life and living. For help in making a list of things to confess and ways to bring Him glory, digest the food for thought found in Matthew 6:24-34; Mark 8:34-38; Luke 12:8,9.

Questionable activities

God-glorifying activities
_____

4. Study Matthew 7:24-29. Have you been trying to find God's will for your life without spending time with Him in consistent Bible reading? It won't happen! Would you like to follow a consistent program of praying/reading the Bible, for a certain time each day?

Yes _____ No _____

How many minutes of each day would you eventually like to spend alone with Him? _____

How long will you spend starting today? _____

At what time of day? _____

(Note: It is altogether possible to communicate with God in fractions of a second. You don't have to pray for hours and hours for prayer to work. On the other hand you can be on your knees for "hours" thinking about the breakfast you had today and not accomplish one thing. The quantity of time is not as important as the quality of your praying. However, if you are to really grow in your praying you will find it extremely helpful to spend time alone with God each day.)

5. List some problem(s) you are facing. Are you ready to ask God to help you, adding, "But I want your will, not mine?" Matthew 6:33,34; Jeremiah 29:11-14 are helpful reading.

6. Have you been honest with God in your praying? As you are praying alone right now, honestly ask Him to show you the very, very deepest desires of your heart.

Some of these desires may surprise you. Are you willing to ask Him to keep purifying your desires and motives? Read Matthew 6:22,23; 15:1-20; Romans 7:14-25; 1 John 1:5-10 devotionally.

7. What is God's will for your life? Write down what you think the main thrust is. Are there other possibilities? Keep them before you as you pray/read John 6:38-40 and Ephesians 1:3-23, asking God to make clear His will for you.

8. Psalm 106:13-15 and James 4:3 are good reading as you think about the following: Have you been impatiently demanding of God something you want? Are you feeling lean in your soul? Ask Him to forgive your impatience and make you to want His perfect will, including His perfect timing.

9. Ask God to draw you ever closer to Himself, and shape your entire life and will to His will for you. In what areas would you like to mature spiritually in this next year? Make a list. Consider 1 John 5:14 and John 15:1-11. Go over your list once more.

10. Read Psalm 37:5. What are you going to do differently? What do you understand more clearly as a result of reading and experiencing this chapter on petitions?

For more information and help in petitioning God, see Chapter 7, "Your Praying Notebook: A Tool to Revolutionize Your Prayer Life," Sections 5 and 6.

CHAPTER SIX

Intercession

"Please, God, help my friend get well!"

If you have prayed like this, then you have interceded for your friend. Interceding is asking God to grant something for another person.

The Scriptures encourage us to intercede for one another: "We have not ceased to pray for you" (Col. 1:9, *NASB*). "Pray for one another" (Jas. 5:16, *NASB*). "For I know that this shall turn out for my deliverance through your prayers" (Phil. 1:19, *NASB*).

How Does Intercession Work?

Intercession—asking God to work in the life of someone else—is the privilege of every believer. God knows everything and is everywhere at once. He can be trusted. It is well said, "He never makes a mistake."

As a Christian you can talk with Him at any time—day or night—during your entire lifetime. He is never too busy to hear you or answer your prayer.

Since He is everywhere in the world, He is with you and at the same time with a friend when any problem arises in the life of your friend. When a friend is in danger, He is there. When a situation threatens the safety of a loved one, He is there. When a dear one is ill even to the point of death, He is there.

No matter what the situation of your family or friend, anywhere in the world, this is how intercession works:

1. You ask God to help your friend (Jas. 5:16).

2. God knows exactly what your friend's situation is. He knows your friend's complete past, and what's more He knows

his complete future. He knows his complete physical, psychological and spiritual needs. And, one more comforting thought, He loves your friend even more than you do (Jer. 29:11-14; Ps. 139).

3. God has a perfect plan for your friend's life. He knows your prayer and answers in terms of what is eternally right (Jas. 5:16-18; Luke 11:9-13).

4. Your friend could ask for God's help himself, but it is also important for you to be interceding on his behalf (Jas. 5:13,14).

5. God will help your friend, but your friend must respond to God's leading if he is to have spiritual victory in this situation (Eph. 1:1—2:22).

When You Don't Even Know How to Ask

Occasionally a situation arises when you may not even know how to pray on behalf of your friend. Scripture provides a solution: "And in the same way the Spirit also helps our weakness; for we do not know how to pray as we should, but the Spirit Himself intercedes for us with groanings too deep for words; and He who searches the hearts knows what the mind of the Spirit is, because He intercedes for the saints according to the will of God" (Rom. 8:26,27, *NASB*).

These are extremely important words for Christians. God, the Holy Spirit, is praying on their behalf with sighs and groans too deep for words.

A young man 24 years of age sat across from me. He had terminal cancer and it was going into its final stages. He was very concerned, for he, a believer, did not have the desire to pray. He was weak physically and had only about eight more weeks to live. I read Romans 8:26,27 to him. The load lifted from his shoulders. He could now allow the Holy Spirit to pray for him; and when he was exhausted or didn't feel like praying, he could call on the Holy Spirit to intercede on his behalf.

God absolutely never abandons you as a believer. There are times when you are confronted with very serious and even critical decisions. Sometimes you can't decide the way in which God wants you to go. You really don't know how to pray. In times such as these you can plead for the Holy Spirit to be interceding on your behalf.

A friend was on the hospital's critical list with a painful cancerous brain tumor. He was an outstanding Christian, a brilliantly successful business man, a husband, a father, and only 46 years old. He was told that he had only a few days to live. As I visited him in the intensive care unit of the hospital, I didn't know exactly how to pray. I felt sick. I didn't even feel like praying; I just groaned inside.

Another friend was in the middle of an extremely complex and hard-to-understand problem. He called and asked if we could have lunch. As we talked, he admitted with tears in his eyes (and he is a praying man), "I'm so confused, I can't even think of words to pray."

In both situations, I quickly confess, I didn't have the first idea what to pray on their behalf. I relied completely on the intercessory praying of the Holy Spirit.

Jesus interceded on behalf of the

disciples. In John 17:15 *(NIV)*, Jesus was praying for them, "My prayer is not that you take them out of the world but that you protect them from the evil one." As He continued His prayer, He included Christians of the future—right up to today:

"My prayer is not for them alone. I pray also for those who will believe in me through their message, that all of them may be one, Father, just as you are in me and I am in you. May they also be in us so that the world may believe that you have sent me" (John 17:20,21, *NIV*).

Jesus is now interceding on our behalf, "If any man sin, we have an advocate (intercessor) with the Father, Jesus Christ the righteous" (1 John 2:1, *KJV*).

Intercession Can Be a
Personal Ministry

Many people have found a satisfying personal ministry in interceding for the lives and needs of others.

A lady in our church spends most of her time praying. She is not praying primarily for herself, but for others. She prays for everyone she knows—servicemen, single girls, young families, teenagers, prisoners, political leaders, and many others. She is contacted by people from all over Southern California, and even other parts of the country, with prayer requests. She, and others, carry on a fulfilling ministry of prayer in which miracles take place and people experience the results of prayer.

I also know a very beautiful young woman, age 30, who is a picture of health. She is very busy and popular. Each morning she gets up an hour early asking God to work His will this day in the lives of her family and her friends.

Does "Just Praying" for Someone Really Make a Difference?

When I was younger I was skeptical at this point. I heard missionaries say, "We were aware that you were praying." I must confess that I thought this was probably a public relations gimmick. The day came when I went to a distant foreign country. I was in a place of danger; yet, I felt very confident, more confident than I normally

would in these kinds of circumstances.
Then it struck me—friends back home had
interceded on my behalf. I felt God
responding to the praying of my friends.
Today I know what the missionary meant
when he said he felt others were praying
for him. It isn't sanctified public relations. It
is God answering intercessory praying!

A young man I know is a part of a
ministry team on a well-known marine
base. In the past three years he has helped
literally hundreds of young marines accept
Jesus as their Lord and Saviour. After they
have accepted Christ, my friend has a
favorite question he always asks, "Who has
been praying for you?" He shared with me
recently that every single person who has
accepted Christ under his ministry was able
to tell him immediately of some person who
had been praying specifically for him. God
answers our intercessory praying.

Have you ever had someone pray for
you personally while you were listening? To
mention you by name? To place your need
before God? Do you remember the release
and warmth you felt? When you pray for

someone while you are with him there comes a sense of fellowship as you stand before God talking to Him about a common concern. Friendships deepen through our intercessory praying. This is important to the strengthening of faith in others. Whenever you feel free to do so, intercede for people while they are with you. It always encourages my soul to hear someone mention my name in their praying.

I know a pastor who has a special program of praying personally for each of the over 3,000 members in his congregation. He sends a letter telling them he will be praying for them during a certain week and asking them to share special prayer requests they may have so that he can pray more specifically. This ministry has blessed both the pastor and the congregation. The congregation has reported that they have felt strengthened because of this time of intercessory praying. At the same time many have said that they, too, were praying for the pastor.

Sometimes a person will flash across

your mind and you ask yourself, "Why in the world did I think of that person?" As these people come to mind, pray for them. They may have a special need. You may never know what that person was facing until you get to heaven. Then God will reveal what changes were brought about through your intercessory praying.

Intercessory prayer makes a very real and specific difference. God acts in response to the praying of His people.

God Does Heal Today. . .

Some people have the gift of interceding for others and seeing God heal them (1 Cor. 12:9). God does heal today. Many Christian scholars agree that He heals in at least four different ways:

1. *God heals through nature.* If you cut your finger, it heals naturally.

2. *God heals through surgery or medicine.* A surgeon can remove a tumor or an appendix or prescribe medicine and healing takes place.

3. *God heals through counseling.* A hospital patient needed blood. She

"suffered great pain from the blood flowing into her arm." The doctors knew, however, that it is physically impossible to feel pain caused by blood flowing into one's arm. She had an emotional problem. I sat by her bed and she poured out her soul confessing her sins. We prayed, and she was given the assurance of forgiveness. I left and the nurse came in and started the blood, which she took without any more pain. There are many emotionally caused problems. When these emotional problems are honestly dealt with, there is healing.

4. *God heals divinely.* This healing takes place without apparent scientific cause. For some reason there is a remission of the disease. Often this comes as a result of praying people who may be near or in another part of the country. There are other times when healing like this takes place and apparently no special prayers were offered. All of these are called divine healing. Sometimes healing takes place over a period of time, other times instantaneously.

In all four methods of healing, *God is at work.*

The business of healing is God's. The Christian should join with Christ and pray, "Father, your will be done." The greatest tragedy is not that of being sick or of failing or of dying. The greatest tragedy of life is to be without God. The greatest joy of life is to know and be in relationship to our God who is Lord of the universe and to share in His glory (Rom. 5:2). Our praying should always be that of seeking God's will in the present and His salvation for eternity.

But—there are some sad experiences that can come from well-meaning but poorly-informed people on the subject of healing. There are those who make you feel guilty about the death of your child or loved one if you do not follow their advice and call in a special "healer." Or, if you should call in the healer and the person is not healed, then someone may say there was not enough faith on the part of either the patient or the family or someone else. Not only is the family facing the crisis, but now their faith is being challenged as being not good enough. These inconsiderate advisors would imply that because of this "second class faith" there is no healing.

It is true that there is Scripture that says one must have faith (see, for example, Matt. 21:22). But Christ raised Lazarus from the dead, and it is doubtful that Lazarus being dead, had faith. I do not believe that Scripture is saying that God's power is limited to the faith of the person who is ill. God is able to do what He wants in keeping with His holy will.

Tears come to my eyes just remembering the father who told me of taking his daughter to a service conducted by a nationally known person whom God has used to bring His healing to many people. Every day for years the parents have laboriously strapped the braces on the legs of their daughter so she can walk on her crutches. These people are full of faith. They know what it means to pray and God has blessed them in many ways. They went to the healing service believing that the Lord could heal their daughter. The testimonies of others around them were glowing; God had healed other people in that service. But, when the father, mother and little girl walked out of that auditorium she was still in her braces and on her crutches. The trusting little girl, having witnessed the miracles to others, asked, "Daddy, why didn't God heal me?" Today, years later, she still puts on braces and walks on crutches. God does not answer *every* prayer according to the way we make our requests.

When someone is very ill or there is a tragic situation, a well-meaning friend or acquaintance might suggest that a certain person who has the gift of healing be called in to pray over this person by anointing with oil and laying on of hands. This is a biblical concept about which we read in James 5:13-15. But very often the impression is given that the healer has such a strong and complete gift from God that the prayer is always answered in keeping with how the request is offered.

My experience has been that this is not necessarily true. A neighbor of ours who had this kind of belief had people come in and pray for her. Her church believed in miracles and healings and they were

claiming God's healing for her. People
came often and prayed. Scripture verses
were read. All the scriptural instructions
were followed. Healing was claimed for the
glory of God. But she was not physically
healed; she died!

The answer to the praying was different
from the request. Our neighbor discovered
the ultimate will of God. She entered into
the fullness of the salvation of her Lord.
She was eternally healed of her disease and
will no more see death (Rev. 21:1-4). Her
prayers were not answered; yet, they were.

Interceding Helps Us See
God's Eternal Will More Clearly

Honest interceding is one of the means
by which we come to a better
understanding of God's will. Interceding
causes us to look beyond our own needs to
what God desires for mankind. God desires
salvation, love, peace, life eternal, and
many other great benefits that are easy to
grasp as we read the Scriptures. Praying
helps us see life from the perspective of
eternity and the eternal purpose of God. At

best, man lives 75 to 100 years, which in the light of eternity is only a smidgeon of time. God desires that we have life and have it eternally (John 3:16). The salvation of souls is the means of attaining this eternal goal. Thus, we see God moving according to His eternal purpose in our present life.

We are to intercede for one another. We are to bring each of our particular intercessory requests to God. Just as our personal requests are to be asked in relationship to God's will, it is vitally important to recognize that even in our praying on behalf of others we are to pray as Christ prayed, "Not my will, but Thine be done."

Sometimes we get the idea that if we get enough people to "gang up" on God in prayer, or if we repeat a request enough times, or plead with greater emotion or volume, that we can get God to change His mind and do what we are asking. This is wrong. God is not our genie or slave waiting to carry out every command or to move according to majority vote.

God acts according to His eternal will as revealed in the Scriptures. We only view life from the limited perspective of a few years. But God knows the end from the beginning. Yet we are to pray. God does act in response to the praying of His people. Is this a contradiction? No! It is a mystery. God responds to prayer, but His response is always in keeping with His holy and perfect will.

Personal Response . . . Intercession

1. Is there anything in your life which needs to be confessed and restitution made so that God can once again answer your praying? Please stop and do it now. Then read James 5:16; 1 John 2:1; and Hebrews 7:25.

2. Read Colossians 1:9 and incorporate it into your life. Within God's will what would you like Him to do for friends who are particularly dear to you? Will you make a list and ask God on their behalf? You may want to ask them specifically how they would like you to pray for them.

3. Read/pray about Romans 8:27-29.

What do you want God to do for each member of your family? Make a list. Make it specific so you will know when He has answered and you will be able to thank Him.

4. Who would you like to see accept Jesus as their Lord and Saviour? Making a list of these people will help you consistently pray for them. Hebrews 7:25 and 1 Timothy 2:1 are applicable here.

5. What would God like to do in the life of your pastor or other staff members at

your church? Make a list. Ask God on their behalf after reading Colossians 1:9 and Ephesians 6:10-20 several times.

6. What would God like to do for the hungry, for the naked, for the sick, for the imprisoned people of the world? Ask Him to do it. Intercede on their behalf, using Matthew 25:31-46 and James 2:14-26 for authority.

7. After reading 2 Chronicles 7:14 and 1 Peter 2:4-17, what do you think God would like to do for this nation? Write your thoughts below:

8. See 2 Peter 2:1-22 and Hebrews 12:1-7. Who is it that really upsets you? Are you ready to ask God to give you His love for them? Write their names below. Next ask God to bless the work they are doing for Him and heal the relationship from both sides.

9. Read/pray through Ephesians
1:16-23 and Colossians 1:9-14. Are you
willing to ask God to burden your heart
with a ministry of intercessory praying? If
so, begin to list all of the needs for which
you can pray specifically until His answer
comes. As you are praying, look
expectantly for the answers to your prayers.

Development of intercessory prayer may be helped by turning
to Chapter 7, "Your Praying Notebook: A Tool to Revolutionize
Your Prayer Life." See Sections 7 and 8.

CHAPTER SEVEN

Your Praying Notebook:
A Tool To Revolutionize Your Prayer Life

How many times have you wanted to pray for something or someone and have simply forgotten? Have you ever asked God for something and forgotten to thank Him when you received it? Or have you, as I have, prayed in such a general way that you wouldn't have known it if God did answer your prayer?

George Müeller, a praying English saint, left us an inspirational inheritance. He left a praying notebook he called "God's dealings with George Müeller." In this notebook are recorded over 50,000 specific answers to prayer.

Keeping a Praying Notebook will revolutionize your relationship with God. It will be a thrilling experience for you. One year, or even ten years from now, you will be able to look back just as George Müeller did, and thank God for His faithfulness in meeting your deepest needs and for providing for you as His child.

Keep your Praying Notebook with your Bible, and when you are communicating with God in prayer and Bible study, write down your praises, confessions, thanksgivings, petitions, and intercessions.

Your faith will grow continuously as you see specific answers to your prayers.

Keeping a Praying Notebook is a little bit like marking a four-year-old's height on the door to his room. When he is five years old, he isn't aware that he has grown at all until he sees the marks and can compare his height with the earlier marks. Keeping a Praying Notebook allows you to experience the thrill of watching how God is helping you grow in your faith.

Each time you meet with God your faith grows stronger. After a few months, look back and have your faith leap as you see how God led you and answered your praying.

Your Praying Notebook can also be

very humbling. When you accomplish something and start to say, "Look what I have done . . . see what I've accomplished," look in your Praying Notebook. You might find it is one of God's answers to your prayers. Then thank Him!

On the following pages are suggestions for how to build your own Praying Notebook. You may use these pages to write in for your first notebook; however you will want to prepare a larger, more effective one as you grow in your praying. A good size is an 8½ x 11-inch three-ring binder.

On the first page of your notebook, you might want to include something like this:

IF LOST—CONFIDENTIAL, Please!

Return to:

_____
Name   Phone
_____
Address
_____
City   State   Zip

Also include an index in your Praying Notebook, which you might organize along these lines:

PRAISE
>   Section 1—Father, help me to see you as you are. . .

CONFESSION
>   Section 2—Father, change my life in these areas. . .

>   Section 3—Father, help me to love these people. . .

THANKSGIVING
>   Section 4—Father, thank you for. . .

PETITION
>   Section 5—Father, what is your will concerning. . .

>   Section 6—Father, I would like these things. . .

INTERCESSION
>   Section 7—Father, please do this for my friends. . .

>   Section 8—Father, please bring these people to a saving faith. . .

You may think of other pages for your notebook as you go along. Some sections will undoubtedly grow larger than others, depending upon your personal needs, interest and spiritual development. The important thing is to get a notebook started and keep it going. There is no time like today to begin recording God's dealings with you!

PRAISE. . .

Father, help me to see you as you are as a result of my study of the Scriptures and praying.

God is. . .	Other notes including references to verses and chapters:

Thank you Father

CONFESSION . . . ● Section 2

Father, change my life in these areas:

Started praying Date	I need to be more like Jesus in these ways:	Answer Date

Thank you Father

CONFESSION. . .   • Section 3

Father, help me to love these people just as you do.*

Started praying Date	Person	Started loving this person Date

Thank you Father

*These people may be your enemies, they may be from the wrong side of the tracks, or, you may just have a personality clash. But for some reason you need extra help in loving them. If there is someone you would rather not start loving . . . put that person on the top of the list.

THANKSGIVING

● Section 4

Father, thank you for*

Date	These!

Thank you Father

*Jesus/ relationships/ problems/ things/ God's work in the lives of others, etc.

PETITION. . .

Father, what is your will concerning these things? I can't seem to figure them out and I need your Help to see your answers.

Started praying Date	Areas in which I need God's direction:	I now see His will clearly Date

Thank you Father

PETITION. . .   • Section 6

Father, I would like these things. In total honesty, I would like to have (desire) or feel the need for these things when you feel it would be best for me to have them. . . . But more than any of these things, I want your will to be done and you to receive glory.

Started praying Date	I would like these things:	Date needed	Answer yes/no

Thank you Father

INTERCESSION. . . • Section 7

Father, please do this for my friends or family. . . . Your will be done—for your glory—in your perfect time schedule.

Started praying Date	Friend's name	Request	Answered Date

Thank you Father

INTERCESSION. . . • Section 8

Father, please bring these friends and relatives to a saving faith in Jesus as the Christ. That day the angels will sing and so will I.

Started praying Date	Name	Answered Date

Thank you Father

CHAPTER EIGHT

The Next Seven Days Will Shape the Rest of Your Life

A great and famous author was asked by a young journalism student, "Sir, what is the key to writing?" "WRITING," answered this wise author. "If you write one hour a day for one year, your writing will be greatly improved."

The same is true with praying. The key to praying is to PRAY! Actually praying. Don't just talk about it or read about it—actually start praying.

Start praying today! You have read this book on praying. You know the basics of praying. The next seven days will shape

your life. If you say, "Oh that's nice but I
guess I'll put off starting until next month,"
chances are you will NEVER start.

If you will work at your prayer life each
day for the next seven days it will set a
direction for your life. This can continue for
your entire life.

During this next seven days decide on a
certain number of minutes that you plan to
spend each day in praying and reading the
Bible, etc. Make this time realistic. Don't try
to spend 10 hours a day for the first seven
days. You would only experience
frustration. A combined reading and
praying time somewhere between 15
minutes and one hour, where you are
totally alone with God, will make a drastic
difference.

Expect to feel awkward! That is not lack
of faith. It is lack of experience. You may
feel self-conscious . . . especially when
family and friends are around. Don't get
discouraged. By the end of the next seven
days you will feel much more comfortable
in your personal praying.

Praying effectively and in a way that

you really enjoy is not natural or easy for most people. In one sense you must *learn* to pray like you *learn* to walk. You may try to start praying regularly and feel that you have fallen "flat on your face." But, just as a toddler does, you get up and start over. One step at a time you begin to walk more comfortably. Just so with praying. You have to start . . . fall . . . get up . . . and start again. . . and you will begin growing in your prayer life!

Your praying will develop day after day . . . week after week . . . year after year. Soon your praying will seem very natural and enjoyable to you just as walking does today.

Ask for faith. During these first seven days it may seem to you like "my prayers are bouncing off the ceiling." The disciples even had this problem. Don't let your lack of faith defeat you. Pray, saying, "Lord, I believe (a little). Help thou my unbelief." If at first it seems that your prayers are getting absolutely nowhere . . . KEEP GOING! Plow ahead for these seven days and God will encourage your spirit.

How to Start and Keep Going

Here are some practical suggestions to help you get started this week.

1. GET A GOOD BIBLE. Spend enough money on it to get the one you want. You may have to skip a few meals to buy it. Don't let money stop you. Get a Bible that you can really enjoy reading. (You may want to ask a mature Christian friend or your pastor to recommend one if you are a new Christian.) Caution: Don't wait to start your first seven days of praying until you get a good Bible. Start today!

2. START YOUR PRAYING NOTEBOOK. This is seemingly simple but extremely helpful. It is a critical step for starting a praying experience that keeps going. It is a constant source of encouragement. It is inspiring to look back a week later and see how much you have grown. It is exhilarating to look back at the end of the year and see how God has answered your prayers. Take this seriously especially during the first seven days. This step alone can revolutionize your praying life.

3. GET A DAILY DEVOTIONAL BOOK. Read it each day for this week. Read it before you pray and it can help you get in a prayerful attitude. Practically speaking, if you are just waking up, you may need to get your entire body awake and your mind and heart thinking about spiritual things.

4. DO THE "PERSONAL RESPONSE" SECTIONS OF THIS BOOK. If you haven't completed these sections this is a helpful place to start spending a few minutes each day. If you don't finish, it doesn't matter. Just do some each day. If you have them done already, simply review them.

5. PRAY ALONE. Praying with people is fine—and helpful—but, learning to pray alone is your primary task. During this first seven days, work at developing your PERSONAL praying.

6. PRAY AT WORK, AT SCHOOL, AND WHEN OTHERS ARE AROUND. During this first seven days instead of "thinking things over" talk them over with God. When problems come you don't have

to pray out loud on the job, but talk it over with Him in the quietness of your heart and mind.

7. PRAY OUT LOUD. You can think prayers in your mind and God hears. But when you are alone with Him, also try praying out loud. It really makes a big difference. It keeps your thoughts from wandering. It helps keep you awake. If you find that others are disturbed or are listening in another room, whisper your prayers. It really does help!

8. PRAY IN THE MORNING FIRST THING. This isn't a hard and fast rule, but it is a helpful one. Give God the first of your day. Pray about the things you are planning. Your week will be different when each day is started with prayer.

9. DRINK SOMETHING HOT OR COLD. It isn't wrong to be sipping a drink while you are praying. It helps you keep awake early in the morning or late at night. At first it is hard to get up extra early. Drinking something really helps!

10. PRAY WITH PEN IN HAND. Write down (in your Praying Notebook) what you

ask God for and watch to see how and
when He answers. Also write down
distracting thoughts that come to your mind
during your prayer time. When your prayer
time is over you can deal with these things
appropriately.

11. KNEEL. You don't *have* to kneel to
pray. God hears you even if you are
standing on your head. But you will find
that as you kneel and bow your body
before God, it helps you bow your mind
and will to Him also.

12. FIND A PRAYER PARTNER. You
may want to talk with a mature Christian
friend and ask him or her to pray that you
will stick with your program for these days.
You may want them to call you at a certain
time each morning. This can help you
develop a consistent prayer life.

Note: If your class or group is studying
this book together, you may want to
choose partners and encourage each other
to keep praying during the first seven days
. . . and beyond.

13. MAKE A LIST OF FRIENDS YOU
CAN ENCOURAGE TO START PRAYING.

Make the list during the seven-day period. When your seven days are up and you are really excited personally about your prayer time, encourage others to start. You may consider giving each a gift of this book. Have them read it and then discuss it with you. As more and more of your friends are praying it will also help your own commitment to praying to remain strong. Note: As you point friends to Jesus and they become new Christians start them first reading the Bible and then praying. (This book was designed to be given as a gift to new Christians to help them get started.)

14. SPEND TIME LISTENING. During the first seven days this will be fun. Try it. Honestly ask God to guide your thinking in the next one to five minutes and then allow Him to bring thoughts to your mind. (Remember: check these leadings with Scripture.)

15. ASK GOD TO HELP YOU WANT TO PRAY. He will answer your prayer if you ask sincerely. Ask Him to prepare your heart to want to keep praying. Ask Him to help you see yourself as a praying person

for the rest of your life. The more you actually pray and start enjoying your prayer time the more it will seem natural to pray. The enjoyment will increase and the awkward feelings will leave.

Don't be ashamed of using some of these practical suggestions as crutches. That's all right. Crutches are sometimes helpful. Use praying crutches to help you pray until it seems so natural and so enjoyable to spend this time alone with your heavenly Father, that you just wouldn't miss it. Soon you will be without "crutches"—you won't need them.

God is everywhere. He is always with you. Tell Him everything. Practice remembering the fact that He is with you even right now. Turn to Him with all problems big and small. Thank Him for everything just as you would any other friend. No matter where you are, simply say aloud or to yourself things like: "Thank you Jesus"; "What do I do here, Lord?"; "Isn't this a beautiful day, Lord?"; or "I love you, Jesus." Praying soon becomes as natural as breathing.

As prayers are answered and victories are won because you have prayed, it becomes easier and more enjoyable to keep going. (Your prayer notebook will help you keep records.)

As you finish your first seven days, start another seven days. Soon your prayer notebook will help you see that you have kept going for an entire year.

Don't Stop . . . Keep Going!

There is a story told that the world famous pianist Ignace Paderewski was giving a performance at a stylish London concert hall. It was about a half hour before the master was expected and already the hall was packed. The electricity of excitement had everyone talking and looking to see the other celebrities in attendance. White ties and long elegant gowns were everywhere.

The only item on the bare platform was one very large grand piano. Spotlights were already focused on the piano bench awaiting the master. One admiring mother had paid the full adult ticket price for her seven-year-old son. She knew he would practice with much more interest if only he could hear the master pianist.

In the gaity of conversation, however, the young lad slipped out of the padded concert hall chair and was gone. His mother soon noticed that he was missing and began looking frantically about the packed auditorium. Then she heard a very strange sound drift out over the immediately hushed crowd.

Her eyes flashed to the piano where she spotted her seven-year-old son. He was sitting on the bench prepared for the master. The spotlights were on him. He was playing. "Chopsticks!"

"Chopsticks!" someone called from the angered crowd. "Get that kid down!"

Terribly embarrassed, the mother started into the crowded aisle, pleading apologetically, "Please, let me through—that's my son."

She was so busy working her way through the crowd that she had not seen the internationally famous master slip onto the stage and sit beside her son.

"Chopsticks" remained very clear in the music that followed. Everyone could hear "Chopsticks." But, the master started to fill in all around the simple tune. He played tear-producing, spine-tingling runs and made the makeshift piano duet into a masterpiece.

By this time the mother was close enough to the stage to hear the master encouraging her son, "Keep going, boy. Don't stop now. I'll help you. Don't stop now. Keep going!"

Often as we are praying we feel as if we are playing "Chopsticks." But our heavenly Father comes to us—in our feeble human effort—and encourages us, saying, "Keep going. Don't stop now. I'll help you. Don't stop! KEEP GOING!"

Notes

1. For a more thorough discussion of this subject, see *Systematic Theology,* vol. 3, by Charles Hodge (Grand Rapids: Wm. B. Eerdmans Publishing Co.), p. 700.
2. For more information on this subject, read *Systematic Theology* by Louis Berkhoff (Grand Rapids: Wm. B. Eerdmans Publishing Co.), pp. 47-51, and *The Doctrine of God* by Herman Bavinck (Grand Rapids: Wm. B. Eerdmans Publishing Co.), pp. 83-110.
3. The Reverend James Hagelganz, co-author of this book, relates the following incident regarding peace of mind: "As I was trying to work on the manuscript for *Praying,* I had an interruption that irritated me. After the person left, I prayed for him. Something happened to me. My irritation left and I felt a sense of compassion. I was able to care about his welfare. I had peace of mind and was freed from my irritation."
4. To bless means to "pronounce as good or favorable; to speak well of." It comes close to the meaning of success or "to make happy."
5. Garth and Merv Rosell, comp., *"Shoe-Leather" Faith* (St. Paul: Bruce Publishing Co., 1960), selection no. 212.

Have you ever wondered . . .
- Why can't I pray more consistently?
- Why is praying sometimes so hard to do?
- Are my prayers getting off the ground?

If you ever have, this book is for you!